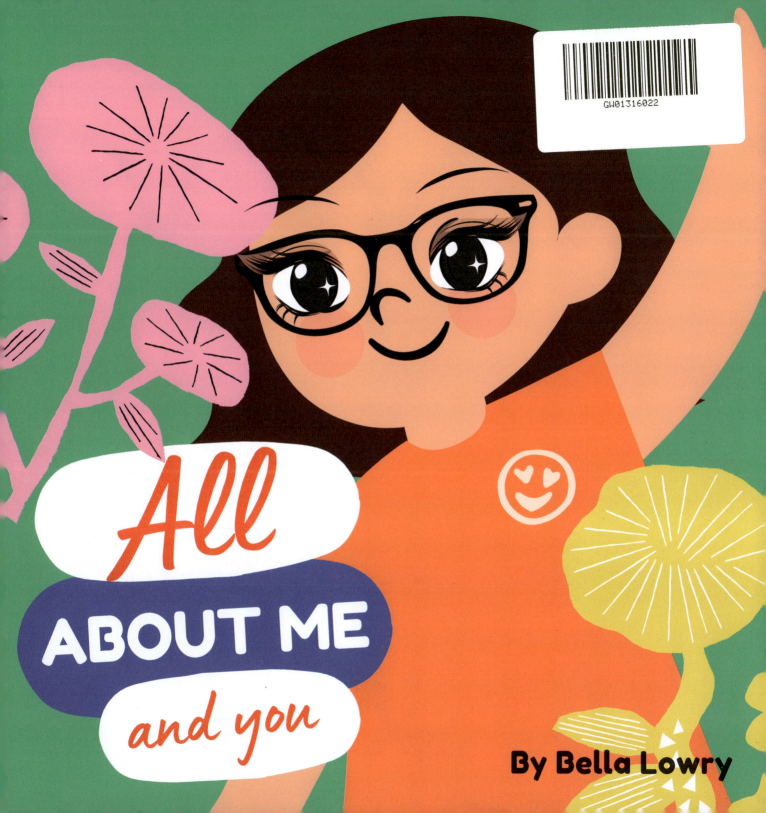

Hi! My name is Bella Louise Lowry and I am 10 years old. I will be 11 in a few weeks. In this book, I am going to tell you all about myself and you can tell me about yourself too. I am looking forward to being your friend!

My Home

My house is grey with a black door. It has an upstairs and a downstairs. I have a garage beside my house, it also has an upstairs and a downstairs. There are lots of things to do in it like playing darts, watching t.v and singing - there is even a bar!

How about you? What is your house like? Write about it on the lines.

And what about you? What are some of your favourite colours? Colour in the circles!

1st **2nd** **3rd**

Do you like pink, like me, or a different colour?

MY FAVOURITE FOODS

1st **2nd** **3rd**

Yummy strawberries! Yummy chocolate! Creamy pasta!

What about you? What are some of your favourite foods? Draw or write the name of them in the boxes.

yum! yum!

1st **2nd** **3rd**

MY FAVOURITE THINGS
SLAY *SLAY*

1st

Music

2nd

Skincare

3rd

Games/videos

How about you? What are some of your favourite things? Draw or write them in the boxes.

1st **2nd** **3rd**

When I Grow up......

When I grow up, I want to have a big house with a swimming pool and four bedrooms. I also want to have two kids, a boy and a girl. My dream job is to be a singer and an actor.

My Dream House

What about you? What do you want to be when you grow up or, what do you want your house to look like and, how many kids do you want? Fill that all in here.

_____

_____

_____

_____

_____

_____

_____

My Family

In my family there are five people and six pets. My Mum, my Dad and my two brothers, Joey and Max. I also have three cats and three fish my cats are called Dolly, Boxy and Dixie. My fish are called Pippa, Joe and Robin.

My Family

Dad/Stephen - My Dad's full name is Stephen John Lowry, he likes building, his favourite colour is blue and his birthday is in December.

Mum/Amy - My mum's full name is Amy Louise Lowry, she likes reading, her favourite colour is pink and her birthday is in October.

My family

My brother/Joey- Joey's full name is Joey John Alexander Lowry, he likes playing football, his favourite colour is red, he is 8 and his birthday is in March.

Me/Bella- My full name is Bella Louise Lowry, I like singing, my favourite colour is pink, I'm nearly 11 and my birthday is in July.

My brother/Max- Max's full name is Max Stephen Lowry, He likes playing with trucks and diggers, his favourite colour is green, he is 5, and his birthday is in December.

My Relatives

My Mum's Side

My Grandparents - On my mum's side of the family I have two grandparents. My granny is called Shirley and my granda is called Desmond. He is usually called Desy.

My Uncles - My mum has two brothers which means I have two uncles on my mum's side they are called Lee and Barry.

My Aunties - I have two aunties on my mum's side, Lee's wife is Julie-Ann and Barry's is Serena.

My Cousins - I have 5 cousins on my mum's side, Barry has 2 sons and Lee has 2 sons and one daughter, Barry's sons are called Matt and Ben and Lee's children are called Luke, Madison and Ethan.

My Relatives

My Dad's Side

My Grandparents - On my dad's side of the family I have two grandparents. My granny is called Jeanette and my granda is called John
(He's my friend Katie's bestie - private joke! haha)

My Uncle - My dad has one brother which means I have one uncle on my dad's side he is called Gareth.

My Cousins - I have two cousins on my dad's side, they are called Abbie and Isabelle. Abbie is 8 and Isabelle is 4.

What is your family like? Do you have any siblings and what's your full name?

my pets

Dixie   Boxy   Dolly   Pippa, Joe and Robin.

Do you have any pets? If you do, write about them on the lines!

My Friends

Lexi- Lexi is my best friend. We have been friends for nearly 9 years, her favourite colour is pink, her birthday is in October, she is 10 and a half and she likes singing.

Katie - Katie is my bestie. We have been friends for 6 years, her favourite colour is pink, her birthday is in April, she is 10 and she likes playing football.

Amelia- Amelia is my BFF. We have been friends for 5 years, her favourite colour is blue, her birthday is in March, she is 10 and she likes Harry Potter.

My Friends

bestie

Ava-
Ava is my bestie. We have been friends for 2 years. her favourite colour is pink. her birthday is in May. she is 10 and she likes Stitch.

Lily- Lily is my BFF. We have been friends for 4 years. her favourite colour is blue. her birthday is in August. she is 10 and a half and she likes football.

Anya- Anya is my best friend. We have been friends for two months. her favourite colour is purple. Her birthday is in November. she is 10 and she likes animals.

I also have some other friends called Aaron, Grace, Zara, George, Rebecca and Charlotte. They are not in my class but some of them go to my Mum's Spanish class 'Amigos De Amy'.

Write about your friends in the squares. Describe them. You could write about their favourite colour or how you met!

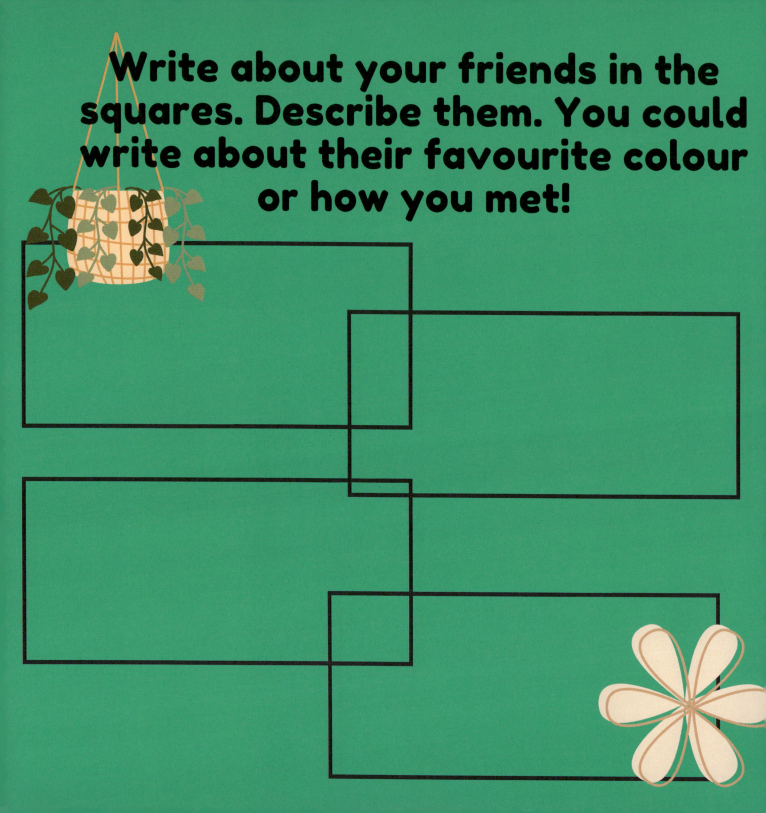

My Hobbies

Singing

Football

Gymnastics

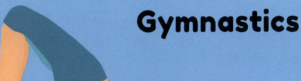

My Hobbies

I have lots of hobbies, because..........

- On Mondays I have football training with Dergview FC.

- On Tuesdays I have Spanish class with my Mum, her school is called Amigos De Amy.

- On Wednesdays I have Drama and Singing class with Much Ado Stage School, my teachers are Rois, Jamie, Samantha and Grace.

- On Thursdays I have Spanish class again with my Mum and Girls Brigade in Garvetagh hall, my leaders are Lauren, Hazel, Shelly and Kyra.

- On Fridays I have piano lessons with Marcella Wright.

Now write about some of your hobbies on the lines! Do you play a sport like me or do you dance?

Cornet - I've been playing the cornet for nearly 2 years, my cornet teacher is Chris Wright and I go to him in school time every Monday.

My Musical Instruments

Piano - I've been playing the piano for five years, since I was five! I got a Distinction in my Step One piano exam. I will be doing Step Two soon.

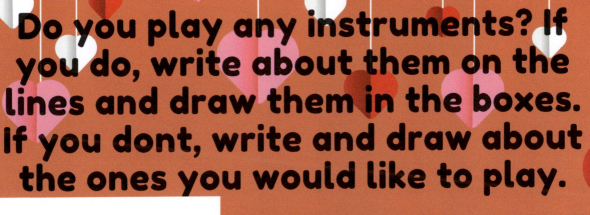

Do you play any instruments? If you do, write about them on the lines and draw them in the boxes. If you dont, write and draw about the ones you would like to play.

 # Singing

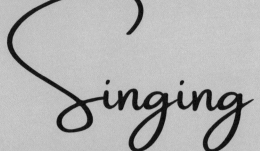

I love singing - especially pop and country songs. Some of my favourite singers are Claudia Buckley, Olivia Rodrigo, Taylor Swift and Morgan Wallen. My favourite song right now is 'I Had Some Help' by Post Malone and Morgan Wallen. My best friend Lexi has recorded and released her own single. How cool is that?!!

I have got Merits in Pop Music Vocals exams up to Grade 3 and a Distinction in Grade 1 Musical Theatre.

I sing with my piano teacher, Marcella Wright and also with my Drama/ Singing teacher Rois Kelly-Lynch. I sing at my church, my school and at Marcella's concert every year. I have performed in Much Ado's productions of 'Annie', 'Frozen' and 'Matilda'.

What about you? Do you like singing? Even if you're not a great singer, you should still sing! It always puts me in a good mood! Tell me about your favourite singers below....

My school

In my school, I am in Year 6, my brother Joey is in Year 4 and my other brother Max is in Year 1. In my class there are 30 people - there are 14 girls and 16 boys.

My teacher is Miss Roke and my classroom assistants are Mrs Sproule and Mrs Turner.

My Class

Girls

There are 14 girls in my class, They are called............ Bella, Lexi, Katie, Amelia, Anya, Ava, Lily, Millie, Scarlett, Alex L, Sophie, Summer, Emily and Jessica.

Boys

There are 16 boys in my class, they are called........ Charlie C, Charlie I, Ben, Masyn, Ollie, Seth, Samuel, Harry, Alex G, Sebastian, James, Jacob, Robin, Aaron, Jenson and Jamie.

And how about you? Tell me about your school, how many people are in your class, who's your teacher and what class are you in?

_____
_____
_____
_____
_____
_____
_____
_____
_____
_____
_____

I hope you enjoyed my book!

Keep looking out for my new series 'My Best Friend Bella'. First book coming soon.......

Printed by Amazon Italia Logistica S.r.l.
Torrazza Piemonte (TO), Italy